To Love Like Espresso

Brandi M. Gomez

BookLeaf Publishing

Presentation by *BookLeaf Publishing*

Web: www.bookleafpub.com

E-mail: info@bookleafpub.com

ISBN: 9789357441032

First edition 2023

TO MY MOTHER, MASHALLE.

A thousand memories and today...

PREFACE

My efforts for the past year feel so deep. I feel like I've reached my filled cup to encourage the animation of my endeavors. But my zest is not the only inspiration to these words that follow. It is my love of words and my comfort in combining them. It is the excitement of creating and reading back my products. It is seeing what my inspiration comes up with after a rush of a written tick. That's what I hope you experience with this collection; A series of ticks and personalities that I embrace of myself. They ponder, lose, win, and feel happiness. Most notably, they are inspired by love, triggers, and various types of coffee.

When the day seems to tire from a long day of work, the sun will have passed its peak and the breath becomes shallow, the first thought is a delicious cup of coffee…

"I Feel"

I feel... still, like a tree stump
But I haven't gotten cut down yet,
And maybe I won't even get there.

I feel something like a bowl of rosemary put together,
smelling so sweet.
Yet I could use a little more mixing,
A little more getting to know more about myself, you know.

I feel... happy, joyous, and appreciated.
Words can't even tell it.
I just know I haven't had a love
Treat me like they do,
And I'd like to keep them forever.

I feel like a new taste of honey,
All wrapped up in a jar,
And I just can't wait to spread my love onto them.

Their body like a piece of toast or
maybe a stack of buttermilk pancakes,
I can drench my heart out onto.

Yeah, I'd like that very much.

I feel like I can be whatever I want,
Take over the world or somethin'
But just while they're in it.

I feel... still, but in a good way.
Their presence keeps my mind from jumping.
From making mistakes and going backwards.

I feel like maybe we were really
meant to be together.
And they really are bringing me together.

I smile writing this because I can't
see anywhere beyond that smile,
their dimples, and adoring personality.

I feel... mmmm.

"She"

She came from an unhealthy
relationship with herself and
unnecessary misconduct.

Unhealthy, the kind where she
didn't feel love anywhere,
not even in her own heart and skin.
And so she abused the outside
to try and feel something on the inside.

Misconduct, she hasn't felt
pleasure in sex since she had her
virginity taken from her.
But then again, she didn't know better.

She implanted the idea that men
don't love, they fuck, and they fuck hard.
They fuck feelings and they fuck our insides.

That's what women were really
looking for when they said they were searching
for love.
The last straw was when she was cheated on.

She thought, if I'm letting you fuck
all damn day, and I'm there when
you need me, why can't it just be me?

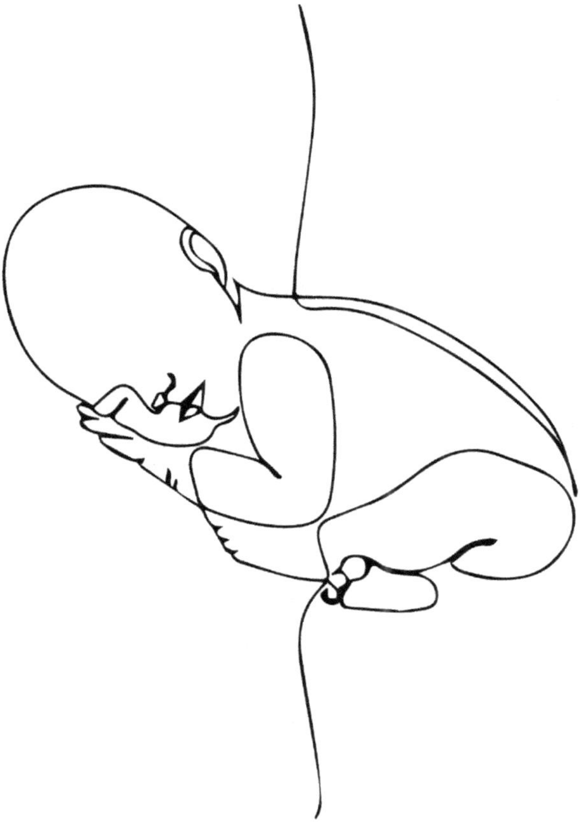

And she realized she had no love in
her under hate.
She was the epitome of hate.

So, she put her soul in the hands of the Universe,
with no idea it'd take it.
She had trusted in empty promises before,
so what's another one?

From then on it was lonely,
sitting and thinking.
She'd been abandoned
by the very thing that destroyed her,
her false self,
because there was nothing to entertain.

The lashes of her self-hate turned into
curiosities.
She whispered prayers to the universe,
ones when she cried and others when she
laughed.

She didn't know if his ears were open
to her tragic and earnest orisons,
but she let time pass.
Loneliness turned into solace and her body felt
clean.

Her dreams became articulate goals,
she wanted nothing more than to go up.

Rise, out of the dirt mixed in
with shattered glass and rocks.

Rise, out of the doubt she had in everything.
Rise, into what she now believed in,
a love deeper than strokes and deeper than casts.

Deeper than thrusts and deeper than masks.
And then everything happens for a reason.

The pain and loneliness ended suddenly,
when she fell in love after fourteen days.

"Venice Walks"

Louis Vuitton handbags and red
bottom heels make their way down
a narrow stone bridge coated pink.

The fall, the spring,
the winter, and the summer.
There is no season
without the sweet smell of Venice.

In Victoria-style teacups it steams.

Those bridges become lover locations,
teacups become souvenirs,
and still the smell of Venice walks.

Accents practice to learn,
and world languages become
the very mouths that kiss the handcrafted edges.

Roses reach out of their own vines
just to touch the toes that pass.

In loving steps,
Venice walks, no longer than
the distance between me and Pluto.

Just across a round wooden table.
Among the orange leaves,
pink blossoms, pearly snow,
and yellow rays.

There is no season without the sweet
smell of Venice.

"Our Secrets"

We have secrets but the good kind.
The kind that we share
when our tongues touch.
They exchange tiny affairs at their
progressive brushes,
And I just love the way she blushes.

The way she smiles and says
'mmm'
Because I'm sure she tastes it too,
the heavenly fortune of 'I love you.'

We have secrets but the good kind.
The kind that we share when we
laugh with each other.
Our heads get closer
and we know there, is where
we are forever supposed to.

We have secrets but the good kind.
The kind that we share
when no one is looking,
because my secrets with her
never fail to lift me.

Glances and hugs
or the whispers we gift freely,
secretly displaying our affection abundantly.

"His Potential"

In the broadest sense,
he attends class, goes to work,
And loves his girl right.
Just like an ordinary satire.

His educators admire his words,
his boss, his humor,
and his girl, his secure soul.

Yet he lives with a mind
that can't swallow the fortune he really is.
His truth is a mockery
to the truth of his brilliance,
And there is no way out.

No way out of this maze of criticism
because he is stuck with shameful pocketing.

Sitting in water with a personality
just as alluring as a post-blooming petal
of prepossessing skin.
But a sad reflection looks back
at him in his mirror.

He is the irony of death still blooming.

Because beyond the tainted,
blooming in the wakes of hope
in unconditional self-love,
lies his great potential illuming.

"Rise"

I've been trying to balance responsibility
and keep comfortable.
I've been trying to give my smiles,
do my work and make sure
I am in line with my life.

But I've been feeling I have lost my grip
of these buildings' corners
and soon I will fall.

I will fall past the twenty floors,
I will fall past the many windows;

One of a woman whose stomach bare scars by twins,
One of a young man who already lives lonely,
And of another who cannot mock me.

I will fall until the sun has escaped my eyes.
The thing that distinguishes between my night and day disappears,
I'll fall until I stand up in dreamlike meadows.

Do you see it?

The way my scars disappear,
The way my ribs cover up flat so healthy,
Or the way my body stays still
amongst the busy dream.

I am back to the rush in front of my eyes.
Almost quickly at sight but slow of time.

My smile has weakened on the inside,
And the line I am supposed to be
aligning has bent itself just slightly.

This building in front of me is rising,
Infinitely rising.

"To Love Like Espresso"

Morning sunrise through a tinted window,
Dust dancing in its rays at my angles this way
and that.

The sound of sips and clinging of glazed clay
act like a comfortable symphony at work.
And there hasn't been a table so stable
in the makings of a shaky setting.

My darling blesses me with their presence
like numerous kegs of coffee.

To love like espresso,
An eminent form showers me with attention
forcing adoring gaze
and feelings addicted to sex.

Through the groundworks of a tinted window,
do they force steam through my closed-minded
coffee beans,
Creating a picture worthy of a clear image.

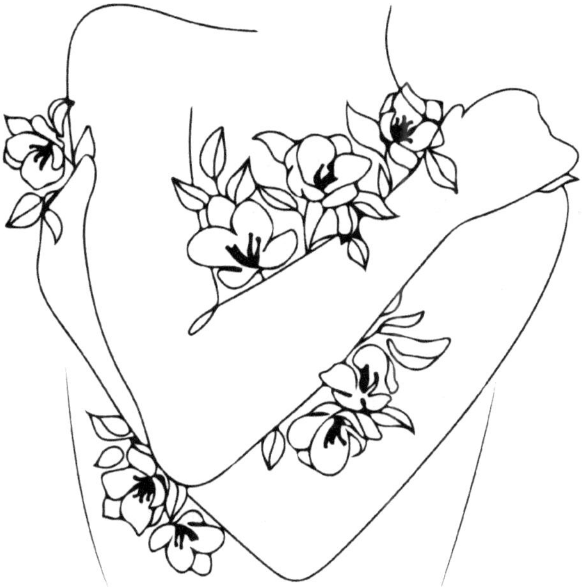

Smiles and sips,
To love like espresso,
Acknowledgements would run in a space of
meaningful conversations.

Taking in the expressed idea of love.
This room is oh so lively.

To love like espresso,
Like to be in love times the amount of cream
added to my black cup of coffee.

"City"

Traffic lights and angry horns
silent the reality of listening.
To be, is a part of the city,
with coded clothing and cloning behavior.

Yet longing bursts in innocent hearts
even before the present visits.

Rushing beings like wiped away paint,
with souls unknown until a couple of coffee
sessions.

It is all in the experience,
the conversation begins to start.

Opening lids to vision commonly dormant
and possible until death.
Unfortunate happenings weigh here
but so do fortunate breaths.

To be a city lit up from within,
by the present moment and true self.
So, make me a skyscraper.

The higher it reaches,

the further the meanings of systems it dealt with.

All around is a beaming lover,
illuminating melanin flashes.
Every moment is taken in by silent wind and
ashes.

Dancing air brushing against cheeks and arms.
Dances created by loved ones.
See and feel the traffic lights and angry horns.

Now further below abiding,
unimportant and so unthought of.
Until hands take hold in meditation,
heart enjoys dependently above.

Consumed in the moment,
right here, right now.
And then a City's distraction is out,
from bitter life's atonement.

"Chai"

Made by boiling the tea and leaves with milk,
A choice of sugar, and cardamom.
A chai to boil up during a cold evening.

Sipping to warm the lips and the body,
Aiding his tone of warmth with mine,
I love the chai he makes with me.

We stir the sugar as if it sings.
Falling to the bottom of a cup,
Sweetening the bitter taste.

A common dose of cardamom.
A dose of love in the morning and dawn.

Chai tea of leaves,
I've never seen it done any other way,
Exactly when I've seen him say...
'It's ready.'

And a smile inches on either side of my face.

No more slump. No more stress.
Because a chai is now upon my desk.

I scoot and sit up in my chair,
Place my hands along the sides of the mug and stare.
Into the cup and there it steams,
My creamy and dull cup of chai.

"Love in a Library"

Unbelievable. The amount of love put out by simple passes on the side of a traffic line. The glances and the smiles, the acknowledgments, and the ignorance. It's all in love.

I've been here for a couple of months now. The city seemed to shrink around me just like its necessities. I walk down a line of living and working and occasionally find myself walking inside the library to and from. But this time it was different.

The feeling of my walk. The pace of my breath and the tingle in my conscious. It was off. The dig of the library entrance pinched my

heart like always but this time,
it was bigger and left a longer
vibration from it to the rest of my
body. My fingers twitched as they
slid across the various book spines.

In the same, I felt the touch just
along my back. I am waiting for
something. My eyes can only see a
collection and so many options, but
my mind understood there was no
choosing today. I walk deeper into
the shop where my eyes force
themselves to see everything.
I can't help but notice a lie.

It dangled in front of my face like a
timepiece made to stop. There were
stories laid out in front of me where
no one truly cared to read except
the occasional bookworm. The lie
was in the time that seem limited.

But there is a story I find worth
reading. It is the man behind the
counter. His light skin and shy face
draw me to him. There is pain
behind his eyes that show me lost
in a world where so many were

fortunate. Brown eyes that are too
bright for the sun outside. The light
above him reflects a raised scar that
reaches from his left jaw to the
right side of his collarbone. I stare
until he becomes nervous. His curiosity
grew and our space now smaller.

There are only movements in our
meeting. No words. It is what the
world around me has become,
strange mouth gestures. Strange
like a broken mime. I point to my
ears and shake my head. Maybe
he'll understand. He smiles and nods
and that was all I need to keep at my approach.

He grabs a notepad that sat close to
him, waiting to be used for an
unknowing introduction. He
grabs a pen that stuck out in his
shirt pocket and pushed. It released
a black tip, and he looked back up
at me. I waited. His finger pointed
to his name tag, worn out and
barely legible, He.
Then his finger moved to the notepad
and raised his pen towards my hands.
I wrote small, She.

"Americano"

A cup of coffee is grounded and
beaten to fit the need for a sip of vigor.

A dilution of espresso by hot water and more.
Oh, what the mixture would do to a cup of
coffee.

It preps, it fixes, dresses itself up.
For a tongue and a sip,
An americano brew for this type of cup.

The taste all battered up,
acquired and slight,
Espresso makes my swill taste right.

The warm you may feel
from stepping out in Texas,
To the smell of a sweet break
and a sigh.

My fit is the making of an
obsession and a fuss,
A fetch at the feel of warmth
and a taste of bitter note lust.

"Cortado"

Steamed but not frothy.
I close my eyes and dream about
what this and that really looks like.

Like a Cortado made
but can't quite put a finger on it...

You know, kind of like my conscience.
The way it reminds me of a good memory,
but the same way it brings on a bad one.

Like a Cortado made,
a purpose to initiate contact
and forbid any feelings out of it.

You know, kind of like my basis.
The way it keeps me grounded in
my boss-like purpose,
but the same way it brings on a consequence.

I'm not interested in the way
my cup is brought to me.
I just like the way I walk towards
the pickup line.

A Cortado made in confidence.

"Tightrope"

Have you ever wondered what it was like
walking on a tightrope?
Well, it's like a long empty pause between being
overwhelmed and the end of it.

It is long. not necessarily in time but in depth.
It's the hot feeling from your head down through
your neck,
and it seeps through your chest down into your
stomach
and then your shaking thighs.
That's how long.

It feels never-ending. I could smile and it would
still be there.
Its depth was the enemy in everything I held
dreamingly.

I was in awe of the spectrum my heart moved
for you.
I made the heat in my body sting through that
tightrope on the inside,
and it hit even on the other side.

I was paused in the feeling.
That is when I noticed it is nothing else but a
feeling.
A temporary feeling, but this one felt like a
series.

The kind you hate to watch on TV.
The nervous tick behind your eyes shuddering at
things
you hear like regrets and goodbyes.

They all matter now at this moment because
your eyes are
wide open, and they can't seem to close
completely shut at night.
This goes on for a week and you still can't
believe this happened
even after a day.

This is what walking on a tightrope feels like.

It's like a broken heart in the middle of rushing
to the hospital.
The long buzz when the heart stops in the
middle of a surgery scene.

And then you come back and tell me you love
me.
The sting and heat shoot up one last time.

The beep of the lifeline comes back responsive.

And just like that, the pause is gone.

"Cold Brew"

Peace is something the world will never reach.
It's somethin' like a looped obstacle
while the finish line sits just outside of it.

Yet there are beings in our societies
in pursuit to teach.
But that is because with self-motivation,
Individuals around the world come together and
sit.

They hum, they chant, and they meditate,
Inside a room of this chaotic world
never-ending,

To search for stillness of their own,
The finish line still in position
outside of their reality,

Like something untouchable and fate cannot see,
We question power and grow curious in song.
Then our lips get chapped as we sing along.

Equality, war, and the title of love grow eerie,
Because what is true alignment in this life
really?

But we could dream what it'd be like if it could be seen.
Peace, something like a glass of cold brew and cream.
Ice cubes dancing and clinking in tune.
The sun kissing our cheeks and then introducing the moon.

But then we come back in terms with a truth existing,
That peace will never be, and it is all still pretending.

Sigh, we are still pretending.

"Take Me"

You were never really mine,
because I was constantly sharing you
with the rest of the world.

And you never made a line between love
and friendship since you proposed.
So, where is the evidence after?

At this point I stand at the forefront with a battle
cry
so that you claim me more than an invisible
string.
I want you to yell my name from the moon
so it would angle down so perfect,
all of the world knew my name that slipped your
mouth.

I want you to cherish me like
roses being given on the first date.
I want a lock on your story to show
your commitment to me without saying my
name.

And even when everyone is around you,
I want you to keep one ear towards me

to hear every second I say 'I love you'.

That you take it every single time,
like a bell ringing across a town in time for
prayer.

Why is it now that my notes are not held in a
jar?
But instead laid out across a lawn of your base
they don't get picked up until you've finally gone
through
these cardboard boxes in your shed.

I'm only asking for a love that says 'I do' in
every chapter.
I'm only asking that you let me be broken and be
my push to
mending my own cracks.

Take me as I am in my flaws to convince my
soul I deserve to live.
Take me so I know I have something to lose if I
go.

"A Thousand Memories and Today"

My favorite memories with you
come a thousand at a time.
They are the scent, the smile,
the roaming warmth you bring to my side.

The older I get the same it feels,
from within to outer still,
every single year.

They are the laughs,
the understanding,
and the unconditional reasons.

I could have been anyone;
From imprisoned by discouragement,
to oppressed by a strict appetite.

But, my mom taught me to be true to the one I only knew.
The one I only knew, and she doesn't come in two.
She may only be construed,
by the very things her mother knew.

They were the advice, the kisses,
and the tending to a small pumpkin patch.

But, her daughter's passion may be mistaken
for a loud mouth that heeds a foe.

Her feelings may be taken unlikely,
Her frame of mind sort of tinted
may have been questioned slightly.

But she stands real tall
with something on her shoulder.
Not the devil or the angel
but instead the one she calls for.

The weight of a ton, the fear to disappoint,
The prayers of her mother.

A thousand memories and today.

They were the shove to never stop or go
backwards.
They were the very essence she brings to move
forward.
They are the love in a single memory,

A thousand memories and today.

"Coffee"

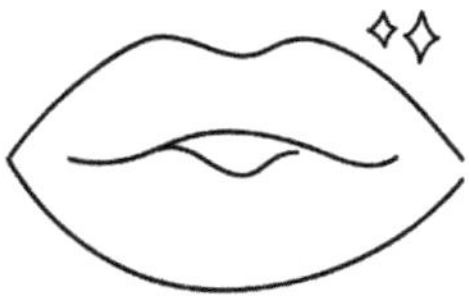

It's unpredictable, life and the feelings that come
with it.
I wouldn't want to be in my head right now;
Vexed and hot coffee drunk, sipping on fuckery.

Do you taste this truth?

It's mockingly sitting on those shivering lips,
peeling from the dedicated bites and nervous
states.
Sticky debris of caffeine makes the stress go
away
and replaces it with soft whistles.

If you haven't been here, visit your local shop,
they are almost at every corner.

Just sit and say what sits between two faces
in unspoken conversations.

The ooh lala of music will drown out
the importance of this meeting if you don't.

And you'll sit there with an unpredictable taste
in your mouth.
Is this what you want?
That ooh lala instead of the swallow?

It's all there in your mind. Like a mirror staring
at you.
Effortlessly, so is a swallow of a black cup of
coffee.

"Hopeful Towards I Made It"

I look at myself in these mirrors and windowpanes and see a reflection of someone I do not know very well. I ask myself 'who are you?' over and over in my head, in hopes it'll make up an answer on its own. I can be still here, looking at this reflection and wish for something not coming, wish for a never-ending love, or a good-paying job I deserve, or even a lifestyle like something out of a magazine. I will always be here still gazing at a reflection unless I decide to move on. I guess that is something I haven't fully grasped. The idea of movement instead of things coming to me. Is it selfish of me to think I truly deserve to move?

I've cried many tears to taste its salty taste. I've smiled wide to feel the ache in my jaws. Yet, all I want now is to move. I've been so still, with figures that my journal entries will be enough, but a skin like mine, brown and pointed out, it will never be enough. I will never be enough. I used to think that if I sweat in my armpits and take deep breaths after my mile runs, after I bent over backwards until my spine can take no more and it sticks out for the world behind me to see, I will be enough. But it is the unfortunate fact that it still will not be enough.

So, is what I dwell my time in worth my efforts? I guess I love being the outsider with a tough obstacle because I won't give up. I love knowing I can do what I want and take the worst way possible because then my doubts are not doubts but instead limits my bias society took hold of. I want to move.

I want to be someone I can look at with blurry vision because my mind and body refuse to stop in motion in such a fast pace industry. That is the way I want my reflection to go. I want to be away from the still gaze and to make it.

And so when I ask myself 'who are you?' I am not referencing the absence of my identity or my ambition. I am referring to the dramatic self-conversation in which I believe everything I work for, I deserve. I grin at the question. I do not investigate the distance with a solemn glare. No, I grin a big grin even when my kinky hair looks messier than usual, and even when my eyes fall away from contact and conversation. I know the work I put out, comes with the accomplishing feeling and hopeful words to say, 'I made it.'

I look at myself in these mirrors and windowpanes and see a reflection of someone I do not know very well. But I know I'll make it. I'll know I've made it.

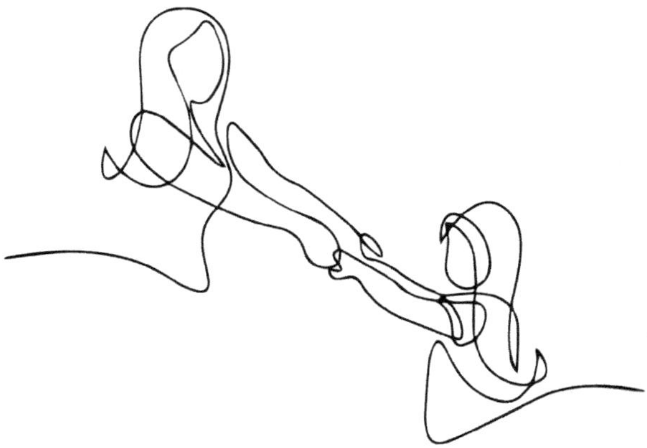

www.ingramcontent.com/pod-product-compliance
Lightning Source LLC
Chambersburg PA
CBHW051741130826
49812CB00033B/952
* 9 7 8 9 3 5 7 4 4 1 0 3 2 *